The Essential Mathematics Glossary II

A Student Reference Guide

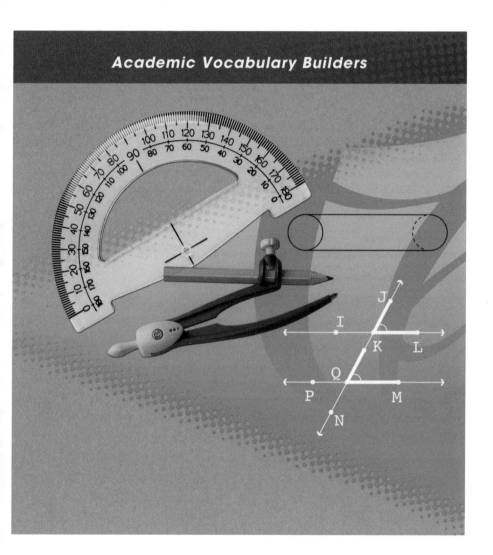

LEARNING

Academic Vocabulary Builders are published by Red Brick Learning
7825 Telegraph Road, Bloomington, Minnesota 55438
http://www.redbricklearning.com

Library of Congress Cataloging-in-Publication Data
The essential mathematics glossary II : a student reference guide.
    p. cm. — (Academic vocabulary builders)
    Includes index.
    Summary: "The Level II glossary covers essential content terms in the key subject
area of mathematics for middle school level students" — Provided by publisher.
    ISBN-13: 978-1-4296-2732-0 (softcover)
    ISBN-10: 1-4296-2732-8 (softcover)
    1. Mathematics — Terminology — Juvenile literature. I. Red Brick
Learning (Firm) II. Title: Essential mathematics glossary 2.
QA41.3.E87 2009
510.1'4 — dc22   2008021057

Cover Design
Ted Williams

Design and Illustration
Heidi Dusbiber

Photo Credits
Capstone Press, cover, i (angle lines, plotting); cover, i (cylinder)
Shutterstock/Caudio Baldini, cover, i (protractor); Dmitry Eliuseev, cover, i
    (drawing tool)

1 2 3 4 5 6 13 12 11 10 09 08

Contents

About this book:

This book will help you learn the essential words you will need to understand to do well on state tests. These essential words will also help you do well in school.

There are about 200 Math words in the book. They are listed in alphabetical order under seven main topics.

Here is a sample word with its features:

Easy-to-read definitions

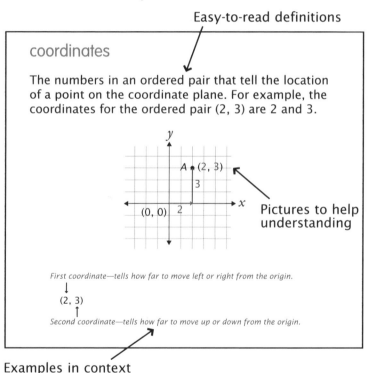

coordinates

The numbers in an ordered pair that tell the location of a point on the coordinate plane. For example, the coordinates for the ordered pair (2, 3) are 2 and 3.

Pictures to help understanding

First coordinate—tells how far to move left or right from the origin.

(2, 3)

Second coordinate—tells how far to move up or down from the origin.

Examples in context

Data Analysis & Probability

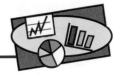

bar graph

A graph that uses rectangles (bars) to display data.

A bar graph compares data sets.

In this example, we are comparing number of votes for each color.

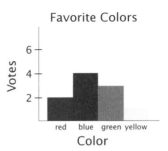

bias sample

A sample where the responses favor some outcomes more than others.

> *Question: Should the school pay for band uniforms?*
> *Bias sample: Ask only students in the band.*
> *Random Sample: Ask every fourth student in the school.*

circle graph

A graph that uses sectors of a circle to display data.

A circle graph shows data as it relates to a whole.

In this example, we are looking at a certain sport - soccer - as it relates to the three sports shown.

Data Analysis & Probability

Geometry & Measurement

Number Sense & Operations

Ratio, Proportion, & Percent

Equations & Inequalities

Variables & Expressions

Coordinate Plane

Reference Chart

Data Analysis
& Probability

Geometry &
Measurement

Number Sense
& Operations

Ratio,
Proportion,
& Percent

Equations &
Inequalities

Variables &
Expressions

Coordinate
Plane

Reference
Chart

combination

A grouping of items in which order does not matter.

Choose 2 people from the 3.

Because you want to choose two people, the order you choose them does not matter.

 *Choosing Joe and Sue is one combination.*

data

Information or facts.

Heights of basketball players, colors of T-shirts, and ages of your family members are all examples of data.

dependent event

When one event happening affects the probability of another event happening.

<u>Event 1</u> – *Pick a green marble without looking in the bag.* Do not replace it in the bag.

<u>Event 2</u> – *Pick a green marble without looking.*

<u>Event 2</u> *is dependent on* <u>Event 1</u> *because the number of marbles changes.*

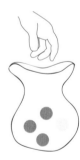

Data Analysis & Probability

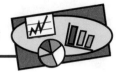

event

One or more outcomes of an experiment. When flipping a coin, an event can be flipping heads on the coin.

experimental probability

Probability based on actual results of an experiment or study.

Age of Students on Soccer Team

Age	Number of Students	Frequency
11	I I I I	4
12	⊬⊦⊦⊦ I I I	8
13	⊬⊦⊦⊦ ⊬⊦⊦⊦ I	11
14	I I	2
	TOTAL	25

There are 25 students on the soccer team; 4 students are 11 years old. The experimental probability of picking an 11-year-old student on the soccer team is $\frac{4}{25}$.

frequency table

A table that displays the number of times each item occurs in a data set.

Age of Students on Soccer Team

Age	Number of Students	Frequency
11	I I I I	4
12	⊬⊦⊦⊦ I I I	8
13	⊬⊦⊦⊦ ⊬⊦⊦⊦ I	11
14	I I	2
	TOTAL	25

A frequency table is best if used to track number of occurrences.

Data Analysis & Probability

Geometry & Measurement

Number Sense & Operations

Ratio, Proportion, & Percent

Equations & Inequalities

Variables & Expressions

Coordinate Plane

Reference Chart

Data Analysis & Probability

Data Analysis & Probability

Geometry & Measurement

Number Sense & Operations

Ratio, Proportion, & Percent

Equations & Inequalities

Variables & Expressions

Coordinate Plane

Reference Chart

histogram

A bar graph that shows the number of times data items occur within certain ranges.

A histogram is best used for data given in ranges.

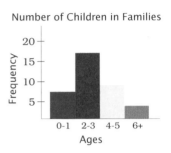

Number of Children in Families

independent event

When one event happening does not affect the probability of another event happening.

Event 1 – Pick a green marble without looking in the bag. Replace it in the bag.

Event 2 – Pick a green marble without looking.

Event 2 is independent of Event 1 because the number of marbles is the same on both picks.

line graph

A graph that uses line segments to show how data changes over time.

A line graph is best used to show change over time.

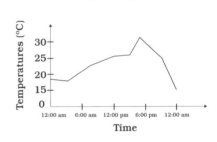

Daily Temperature

Data Analysis & Probability

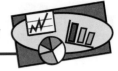

line plot

A number line with symbols above each group to indicate the number of data items in the group.

Xs or other shapes can be used.

A line plot is best used to show number of data in each group.

Cats in Home

```
                    x
      x    x    x    x
      x    x    x    x
   ◄──┼────┼────┼────┼──►
      0    1    2    3    4 or more
```

Number of cats in home

lower quartile

The median of the lower "half" of a set of data.

Q₁ is used to abbreviate the lower quartile.

$$Q_1$$
Lower Quartile

1, 3, ④, 5, 5, ⬚6,⬚ 7, 7, 8, 8, 8

Lower half of data   Median

mean

The sum of the numbers in a set of data divided by the number of numbers in that set.

DATA: 4, 2, 7, 7, 3, 1

Sum of numbers: 4 + 2 + 7 + 7 + 3 + 1 = 24
Number of numbers in set: 6
Mean: 24 ÷ 6 = 4

The mean is sometimes called the arithmetic average or average.

Data Analysis & Probability

Geometry & Measurement

Number Sense & Operations

Ratio, Proportion, & Percent

Equations & Inequalities

Variables & Expressions

Coordinate Plane

Reference Chart

median

The middle data value when a set of data is arranged from least to greatest.

Example A: 4, 2, 7, 8, 3
Arrange the values from least to greatest. 4 is the median.

2, 3, (4), 7, 8
↑
Median

Example B: 9, 4, 7, 3, 5, 8
Arrange the values from least to greatest.

3, 4, 5, 7, 8, 9
↑
Middle Values
Average: 5 + 7 = 12;
12 ÷ 2 = 6
6 is the median.

When there is an even number of numbers, the median will be the mean of the two middle numbers.

mode

The number or numbers that occur most often in a set of data.

Example A: 3, 5, 9, 8, 7, 6, 7
Mode: 7 (It occurs twice.)

Example B: 3, 4, 5, 3, 7, 4, 8
Modes: 3 and 4 (Each occurs twice.)

Example C: 2, 9, 5, 6, 4
Mode: none (No value occurs more than once.)

Data Analysis & Probability

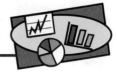

Data Analysis & Probability

Geometry & Measurement

Number Sense & Operations

Ratio, Proportion, & Percent

Equations & Inequalities

Variables & Expressions

Coordinate Plane

Reference Chart

outcome

Any of the possible results that can happen in a probability experiment.

The outcomes are picking a green marble or picking a yellow marble.

outlier

A data point that is very different from other data in a group.

A survey of the teachers' ages at a local school showed the following results:

24, 24, 26, 30, 32, 36, 40, 65
Age 65 is the outlier.

permutation

A grouping of items in which order matters.

Joe　Sue　Ed

You want to choose a president and vice president.

  or
Joe　　　Sue　　　　　　Sue　　　Joe

president　vice president　　　president　vice president

Because you want to choose 2 people for different positions, order does matter.

  or
Joe　Sue　　　　Sue　Joe

Joe and Sue or Sue and Joe are two permutations.

7

population

The entire group to be studied.

All the students in a school are the school's student population.

probability

A number that describes how likely an event is to occur.

The probability of picking a green marble is $\frac{3}{4}$ because there are 3 green marbles and 4 marbles total.

random sample

A sample where every member in a population has an equal chance of being selected for the purposes of a study.

If the names of all the students in a class are put in a hat, and 4 names are selected without looking, then those 4 names make up a random sample for the class. The class is the population.

range

The difference between the greatest data value and the least data value in a set of data.

Data: 14, 16, 16, 19, 21, 24, 28, 28, 35

> *Greatest Data Value:* 35
> *Least Data Value:* 14
> *Range:* 35 – 14 = 21

Data Analysis & Probability

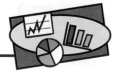

sample

A part of the population used for a study.

Population: All the students in your school.
Sample: Ten students from your school.

scatter plot

A graph that displays two sets of data as ordered pairs.

A scatter plot is used to see if there is a relationship between the two sets of data.

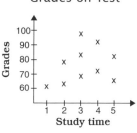

set

A collection of things.

{ 1, 2, 3 }
{ A, B, C }
{ ☆ ◆ ▲ }

stem-and-leaf plot

A data display that uses place value to break apart data values.

A stem-and-leaf plot is often used to organize large data sets.

The ages of the teachers are 28, 29, 31, 32, 32, 41, 43, 50.

Teacher Ages

Stem	Leaf
2	8 9
3	1 2 2
4	1 3
5	0

2|8 = 28 years old

Data Analysis & Probability

Geometry & Measurement

Number Sense & Operations

Ratio, Proportion, & Percent

Equations & Inequalities

Variables & Expressions

Coordinate Plane

Reference Chart

tree diagram

An organized display of all possible combinations or outcomes.

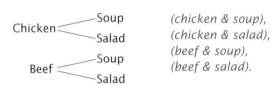

Lunch Choices

Chicken — Soup, Salad
Beef — Soup, Salad

The 4 possible combinations shown are:

(chicken & soup),
(chicken & salad),
(beef & soup),
(beef & salad).

upper quartile

The median of the upper "half" of a set of data.

The upper quartile can be written as Q_3.

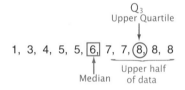

Q_3
Upper Quartile

1, 3, 4, 5, 5, 6, 7, 7, 8, 8, 8

Median   Upper half of data

Venn diagram

A diagram that shows how groups are related.

School Teams

soccer   baseball

Sara   Megan   Pilar
Paul   Elana   Mike

both

Sara and Paul are just on the soccer team.

Megan and Elana are on both the soccer and baseball teams.

Pilar and Mike are just on the baseball team.

Geometry & Measurement

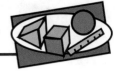

acute angle

An angle that is greater than 0° and less than 90°.

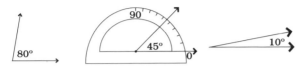

acute triangle

A triangle with each angle less than 90°.

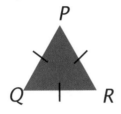

adjacent angles

Angles that have a common point and a common side.

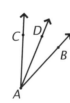

∠CAD and ∠DAB are adjacent angles.

∠CAD is adjacent to (next to) ∠DAB.

Data Analysis
& Probability

Geometry &
Measurement

Number Sense
& Operations

Ratio,
Proportion,
& Percent

Equations &
Inequalities

Variables &
Expressions

Coordinate
Plane

Reference
Chart

Geometry & Measurement

angles

Figures formed by two
rays that have the same
endpoint.

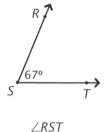

∠ *stands for "angle."*
m∠ *stands for "the measure
of an angle."*

∠*P*   ∠*RST*

m∠*P* = 20°   *m*∠*RST* = 67°

area

The number of square units needed to fill the space inside a
two-dimensional figure.

*Area is measured in square units such as square inches (in.²) or
square meters (m²).*

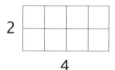

The area of the rectangle is 8 square units.

base (of a solid figure)

A flat surface of a solid figure that helps to describe the type
of solid figure.

The base of a cone is a circle.

base of a cone

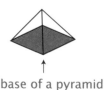

The base of a square pyramid is a square.

base of a pyramid

Data Analysis & Probability

Geometry & Measurement

Number Sense & Operations

Ratio, Proportion, & Percent

Equations & Inequalities

Variables & Expressions

Coordinate Plane

Reference Chart

Geometry & Measurement

capacity

The amount a container can hold.

The capacity for this container is 1 quart.

center (of a circle)

The point that is the same distance from every point on a circle.

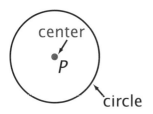

circle

The set of points that are all the same distance from a single point called the center.

The symbol ⊙ is used for "circle."
Circles are named by their centers.

This is ⊙G. Every point on ⊙G
is 5 units from the center.

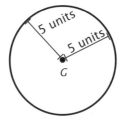

circumference

The distance around a circle.

The letter C stands for circumference.

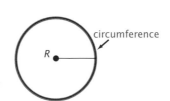

Data Analysis & Probability

Geometry & Measurement

Number Sense & Operations

Ratio, Proportion, & Percent

Equations & Inequalities

Variables & Expressions

Coordinate Plane

Reference Chart

complementary angles

Two angles whose measures add to 90°.

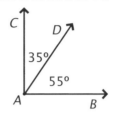

35° + 55° = 90°

∠CAD and ∠DAB are complementary.

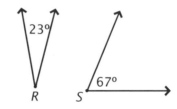

23° + 67° = 90°

∠R and ∠S are complementary.

cone

A solid with one circular base and a vertex.

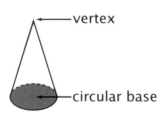

vertex

circular base

congruent

Having the same size and shape.

The symbol ≅ is read "is congruent to."

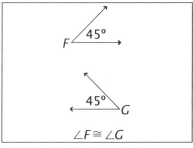

$$\angle F \cong \angle G$$

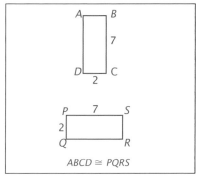

$$ABCD \cong PQRS$$

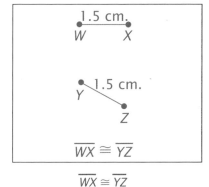

$$\overline{WX} \cong \overline{YZ}$$

Data Analysis & Probability

Geometry & Measurement

Number Sense & Operations

Ratio, Proportion, & Percent

Equations & Inequalities

Variables & Expressions

Coordinate Plane

Reference Chart

15

corresponding angles (of paired polygons)

Matching angles of polygons.

Corresponding angles have the same measure and are in the same position in each polygon.

∠B and ∠F,
∠A and ∠E,
∠C and ∠G,
∠D and ∠H
are corresponding angles.

corresponding angles (of lines)

Angles that are in matching positions when a line intersects two other parallel lines.

∠JKL and ∠JQM,
∠LKN and ∠MQN,
∠JKI and ∠JQP,
∠IKN and ∠PQN
are corresponding angles.

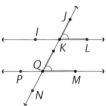

cube

A solid figure with six congruent square faces.

customary system

A system for measuring length, capacity, weight, and temperature.

Some basic units of a customary system are:
Inch (in.)
Cup (c)
Pound (lb)
Degree Fahrenheit (°F)

cylinder

A solid figure with two parallel bases that are congruent circles.

circular bases

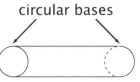

degree (angles)

A unit used to measure angles.

The symbol for degree is °.

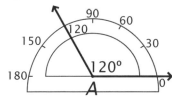

The measure ∠A is 120 degrees or 120°.

diameter

A line segment that passes through the center of a circle and has endpoints on the circle.

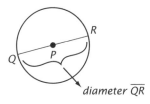

diameter $\overline{QR}$

$\overline{QR}$ *is a diameter of circle P.*

Data Analysis & Probability

Geometry & Measurement

Number Sense & Operations

Ratio, Proportion, & Percent

Equations & Inequalities

Variables & Expressions

Coordinate Plane

Reference Chart

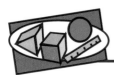
edge

Where two faces of a solid figure meet.

$\overline{BC}$ is one of the edges on this cube. Others are $\overline{AD}$, $\overline{DC}$, $\overline{AF}$, $\overline{AB}$, $\overline{FE}$, $\overline{CG}$, $\overline{EG}$, $\overline{BE}$, $\overline{FH}$, $\overline{HD}$, and $\overline{HG}$.

equilateral triangle

A triangle with three equal sides.

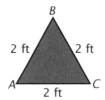

$\triangle ABC$ is an equilateral triangle.

face (of a solid figure)

A flat surface of a solid figure.

ABEF is a face of this cube.

Other faces are ABCD, BCGE, HFEG, DCGH, and ADHF.

hexagon

A polygon with six sides.

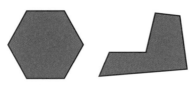

18

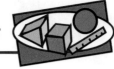

hypotenuse

The longest side of a right triangle. The hypotenuse is the side opposite the right angle.

right angle

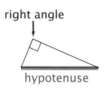

image

The figure formed by a transformation.

Image is a reflection of the original.

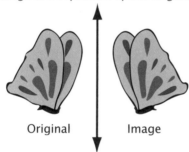

Original   Image

intersecting lines

Lines that meet in one point.

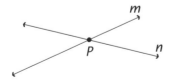

m and n are intersecting lines.

They meet at point P.

Data Analysis & Probability

Geometry & Measurement

Number Sense & Operations

Ratio, Proportion, & Percent

Equations & Inequalities

Variables & Expressions

Coordinate Plane

Reference Chart

Data Analysis & Probability

Geometry & Measurement

Number Sense & Operations

Ratio, Proportion, & Percent

Equations & Inequalities

Variables & Expressions

Coordinate Plane

Reference Chart

isosceles triangle

A triangle with at least two equal sides.

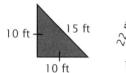

legs (of a right triangle)

The two shorter sides of a right triangle.

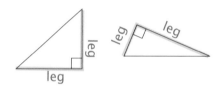

length

The distance of something from beginning to end.

The length of the trip to the school is 2 miles.

line

A collection of points that form a never-ending straight path in opposite directions.

This line is named $\overleftrightarrow{AB}$, read "line AB."

This line is named q.

Geometry & Measurement

line of symmetry

Any line that can divide a figure into two mirrored, congruent parts.

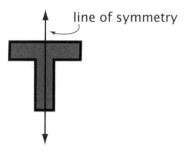

line of symmetry

line segment

The part of a line that connects two points.

A _____ B

Y
$1\ in.$
Z
$\overline{YZ} = 1\ inch$

metric system

A system of measuring based on the decimal system.

Some basic units of a
metric system are:
 Meter
 Liter
 Gram
 Degree Celsius (°C)

Data Analysis
& Probability

Geometry &
Measurement

Number Sense
& Operations

Ratio,
Proportion,
& Percent

Equations &
Inequalities

Variables &
Expressions

Coordinate
Plane

Reference
Chart

net

A two-dimensional figure that can be folded to form a solid figure.

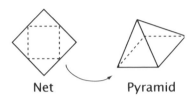

Net   Pyramid

obtuse angle

An angle with a measure greater than 90° and less than 180°.

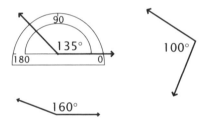

obtuse triangle

A triangle with one obtuse angle.

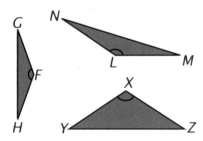

octagon

A polygon with eight sides.

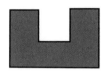

parallel lines

Lines in the same plane that never meet.

The symbol ∥ is read "is parallel to."

 *p ∥ m is read "Line p is parallel to line m."*

 $\overleftrightarrow{ab} \parallel \overleftrightarrow{yz}$ *is read "Line AB is parallel to line YZ."*

parallelogram

A quadrilateral with two pairs of parallel sides.

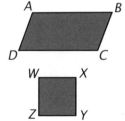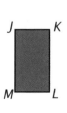

$\overline{AB} \parallel \overline{DC}$ $\overline{AD} \parallel \overline{BC}$

$\overline{WX} \parallel \overline{ZY}$ $\overline{WZ} \parallel \overline{XY}$

$\overline{JK} \parallel \overline{ML}$ $\overline{JM} \parallel \overline{KL}$

Data Analysis & Probability

Geometry & Measurement

Number Sense & Operations

Ratio, Proportion, & Percent

Equations & Inequalities

Variables & Expressions

Coordinate Plane

Reference Chart

pentagon

A polygon with five sides.

perimeter

The distance around a polygon.

The letter p usually stands for perimeter.
To find the perimeter of a polygon, add the lengths of all the sides.

6 + 6 + 4 + 4 + 4 = 24 inches

perpendicular lines

Two lines that intersect to form a 90°, or a right angle.

The symbol ⊥ is read "is perpendicular to."

t ⊥ s Line *t* is perpendicular to line *s*.

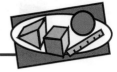

pi

The ratio of the circumference of a circle to the length of its diameter.

The symbol for pi is π.
$\pi = 3.14159....$
The estimated values for pi are 3.14 and $\frac{22}{7}$.

Data Analysis & Probability

Geometry & Measurement

plane

A flat surface with no thickness that extends forever in all directions.

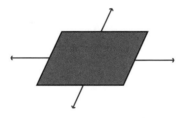

Think of the surface of your desk extending in all directions.

Number Sense & Operations

Ratio, Proportion, & Percent

point

A location that has no size.

Equations & Inequalities

Variables & Expressions

polygon

A closed figure formed by three or more line segments that do not cross (or intersect).

Coordinate Plane

Reference Chart

Data Analysis & Probability

Geometry & Measurement

Number Sense & Operations

Ratio, Proportion, & Percent

Equations & Inequalities

Variables & Expressions

Coordinate Plane

Reference Chart

polyhedron

A three-dimensional solid figure in which all the faces are polygons.

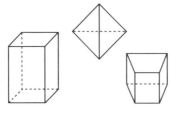

prism

A three-dimensional solid with one pair of congruent, parallel, polygon faces.

A prism is named for the shape of its base.

| triangular prism | rectangular prism | trapezoidal prism |

pyramid

A three-dimensional solid with triangular faces that meet at a point called a vertex.

square pyramid

hexagonal pyramid

Pyramids are named for the shape of their bases.

Geometry & Measurement

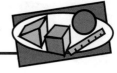

Pythagorean theorem

In any right triangle, the sum of the squares of the lengths of the legs is equal to the square of the length of the hypotenuse.

$$a^2 + b^2 = c^2$$

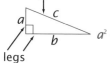

legs

$$a^2 + b^2 = c^2$$

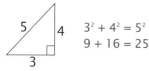

$$3^2 + 4^2 = 5^2$$
$$9 + 16 = 25$$

quadrilateral

A polygon with four sides.

radius

A line segment that connects the center to the circle.

The letter r is typically used to represent the length of the radius.

$r = 2$ inches
$\overline{MG}$ *is the radius of circle M.*

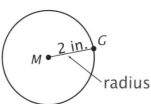

Data Analysis & Probability

Geometry & Measurement

Number Sense & Operations

Ratio, Proportion, & Percent

Equations & Inequalities

Variables & Expressions

Coordinate Plane

Reference Chart

ray

A part of a line that starts at one endpoint and extends forever in one direction.

The symbol for a ray is →.

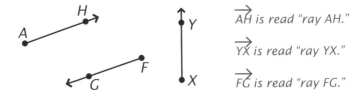

$\overrightarrow{AH}$ *is read "ray AH."*

$\overrightarrow{YX}$ *is read "ray YX."*

$\overrightarrow{FG}$ *is read "ray FG."*

rectangle

A parallelogram with four right angles.

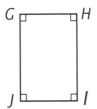

reflection

A transformation that flips a figure over a line to produce a mirror image.

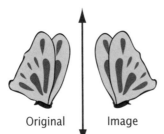

Original   Image

A reflection is sometimes called a flip.

Data Analysis & Probability

Geometry & Measurement

Number Sense & Operations

Ratio, Proportion, & Percent

Equations & Inequalities

Variables & Expressions

Coordinate Plane

Reference Chart

Geometry & Measurement

regular polygon

A polygon in which all sides are the same measure and all angles are the same measure.

Data Analysis & Probability

Geometry & Measurement

Number Sense & Operations

Ratio, Proportion, & Percent

Equations & Inequalities

Variables & Expressions

Coordinate Plane

Reference Chart

rhombus

A parallelogram with four sides of equal length.

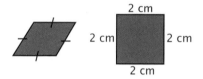

right angle

Any angle with a measure of 90°.

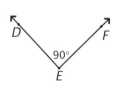

$m\angle A = 90°.$
$m\angle DEF = 90°.$

The measure of angle A is 90°.
The measure of angle DEF is 90°.

29

right triangle

A triangle with one right angle.

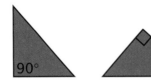

rotation

A transformation that turns a figure about a fixed point.

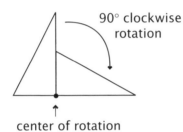

90° clockwise rotation

center of rotation

A rotation is also sometimes called a turn.

rotational symmetry

The ability to turn a figure less than 360° around the center and match the original figure.

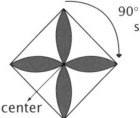

90° rotational symmetry

center

This figure has rotational symmetry.

scale factor

The ratio of corresponding lengths for similar figures.

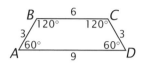

The scale factor of ABCD to NPQM is 3:4 or $\frac{3}{4}$.

scalene triangle

A triangle with no sides of the same length.

similar figures

Two figures with congruent corresponding angles and proportional corresponding side lengths.

The symbol ~ is read "is similar to."

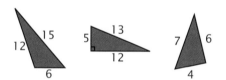

ABCD ~ NPQM is read "ABCD is similar to NPQM."

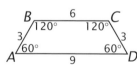

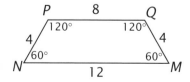

Data Analysis & Probability

Geometry & Measurement

Number Sense & Operations

Ratio, Proportion, & Percent

Equations & Inequalities

Variables & Expressions

Coordinate Plane

Reference Chart

31

Data Analysis
& Probability

Geometry &
Measurement

Number Sense
& Operations

Ratio,
Proportion,
& Percent

Equations &
Inequalities

Variables &
Expressions

Coordinate
Plane

Reference
Chart

skew lines

Lines that lie in different planes and are neither parallel nor intersecting.

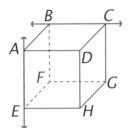

$\overleftrightarrow{BC}$ and $\overleftrightarrow{AE}$ are one pair of skew lines.

sphere

The set of all points in space that are the same distance from a given point (center).

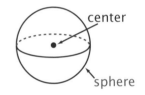

square

A parallelogram with four right angles and four congruent sides.

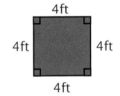

straight angle

Any angle with a measure of 180º.

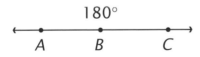

A line forms a straight angle.

Geometry & Measurement

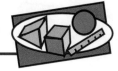

supplementary angles

Two angles whose measures add to 180°.

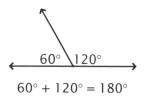

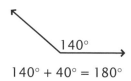

$60° + 120° = 180°$

$140° + 40° = 180°$

surface area

The sum of the areas of all the surfaces.

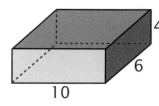

Top: $6 \times 10 = 60$
Bottom: $6 \times 10 = 60$
Front: $10 \times 4 = 40$
Back: $10 \times 4 = 40$
Sides: $4 \times 6 = 24$

$60 + 60 + 40 + 40 + 24 + 24 = 248$ square units
Surface area = 248 square units

tessellation

A repeating pattern of shapes that completely covers a plane.

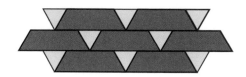

Data Analysis & Probability

Geometry & Measurement

Number Sense & Operations

Ratio, Proportion, & Percent

Equations & Inequalities

Variables & Expressions

Coordinate Plane

Reference Chart

Data Analysis & Probability

Geometry & Measurement

Number Sense & Operations

Ratio, Proportion, & Percent

Equations & Inequalities

Variables & Expressions

Coordinate Plane

Reference Chart

transformation

A change in position, shape, or size of a figure.

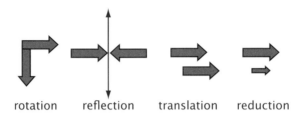

rotation   reflection   translation   reduction

translation

A transformation that slides each point of a figure the same distance and in the same direction.

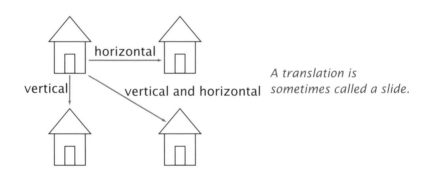

horizontal

vertical

vertical and horizontal

A translation is sometimes called a slide.

trapezoid

A quadrilateral with only one pair of parallel sides.

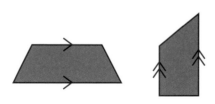

triangle

A polygon with three sides.

vertex

The point of intersection of sides at their endpoints.

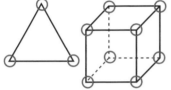

Each vertex is circled.

vertical angles

Angles formed by two intersecting lines.

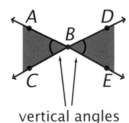

vertical angles

∠ABC and ∠DBE are vertical angles.
∠CBE and ∠ABD are also vertical angles.

volume

The number of cubic units needed to fill the space inside a three-dimensional solid.

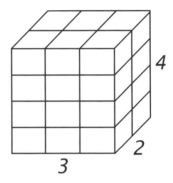

Volume = L (length) 3 × (width) 3 × (height)
V = 3 × 2 × 4 = 24 cubic units

weight

A measure that tells how heavy something is.

The weight of a book is 2 pounds.

Data Analysis & Probability

Geometry & Measurement

Number Sense & Operations

Ratio, Proportion, & Percent

Equations & Inequalities

Variables & Expressions

Coordinate Plane

Reference Chart

Number Sense & Operations

absolute value

The distance a number is from zero (0) on a number line.

The symbol $|\quad|$ is read "the absolute value of."

The number 3 is 3 units from zero on the number line.
$|3| = 3$ *The absolute value of 3 is 3.*

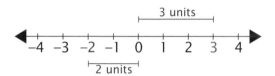

The number –2 is 2 units away from zero on the number line.
$|-2| = 2$ *The absolute value of –2 is 2.*

Associative Property of Addition

For three or more numbers, their sum is always the same. It does not matter how the numbers are grouped.

$(4 + 2) + 8 = 4 + (2 + 8)$
$\quad 6 \quad + 8 = 4 + \quad 10$
$\quad\quad 14 = 14$ ✔

In algebraic notation, this property is written:
For any numbers a, b, and c,
$(a + b) + c = a + (b + c)$.

Associative Property of Multiplication

For three or more numbers, their product is always the same. It does not matter how the numbers are grouped.

$(2 \times 5) \times 8 = 2 \times (5 \times 8)$
$\quad 10 \quad \times 8 = 2 \times \quad 40$
$\quad\quad 80 = 80$ ✔

In algebraic notation, this property is written:
For any numbers a, b, and c, $(ab)c = a(bc)$.

Data Analysis & Probability

Geometry & Measurement

Number Sense & Operations

Ratio, Proportion, & Percent

Equations & Inequalities

Variables & Expressions

Coordinate Plane

Reference Chart

base (of an exponent)

A number that is used as a factor. (The exponent tells how many times to use the base as a factor.)

The exponent is 4.
The base 3 is used as a factor 4 times.

$$3^4 = 3 \times 3 \times 3 \times 3 = 81$$

common factor

A number that is a factor of two or more numbers.

Factors of 8: <u>1</u>, <u>2</u>, <u>4</u>, 8
Factors of 12: <u>1</u>, <u>2</u>, 3, <u>4</u>, 6, 12
Common factors of 8 and 12: 1, 2, 4

Commutative Property of Addition

Numbers can be added in any order without changing the answer.

$$3 + 5 = 5 + 3$$
$$8 = 8 ✔$$

This property is written algebraically as:
For any numbers a and b, $a + b = b + a$.

Commutative Property of Multiplication

Numbers can be multiplied in any order without changing the answer.

$$3 \times 5 = 5 \times 3$$
$$15 = 15 ✔$$

This property is written algebraically as:
For any numbers a and b, $a \times b = b \times a$.

Number Sense & Operations

compatible numbers

Numbers that make calculation easy.

You can estimate using compatible numbers.
120 and 6 are compatible numbers. 120 ÷ 6 = 20.
To estimate 125 ÷ 5.8, you can use compatible numbers.

$$120 \div 6 = 20, \qquad So, 125 \div 5.8 \approx 20.$$

composite numbers

Whole numbers greater than 1 that have more than two whole number factors.

Composite numbers: 4, 6, 9
Factors of 4: 1, 2, 4 because 1 × 4 = 4; 2 × 2 = 4
Factors of 6: 1, 2, 3, 6 because 1 × 6 = 6; 2 × 3 = 6
Factors of 9: 1, 3, 9 because 1 × 9 = 9; 3 × 3 = 9

denominator

$$\frac{3}{4} \leftarrow denominator$$

The bottom number in a fraction.

difference

$$6 - 2 = 4$$

The answer to a subtraction problem   *difference*

Distributive Property

Multiply a single term by two or more terms inside parentheses.
For any numbers a, b, and c, this property is written algebraically in two forms:

$$a(b + c) = a \times b + a \times c$$
$$3(4 + 5) = 3 \times 4 + 3 \times 5$$
$$3 \quad (9) \quad = 12 \quad + \quad 15$$
$$27 \quad = \quad 27$$

$$a(b - c) = a \times b - a \times c$$
$$3(6 - 2) = 3 \times 6 - 3 \times 2$$
$$3 \quad (4) \quad = 18 \quad - \quad 6$$
$$12 \quad = \quad 12$$

Data Analysis & Probability

Geometry & Measurement

Number Sense & Operations

Ratio, Proportion, & Percent

Equations & Inequalities

Variables & Expressions

Coordinate Plane

Reference Chart

divisible

Can be divided by a number with no remainder.

6 *is divisible by* 3.　　　　$6 \div 3 = 2$ *remainder* 0
7 *is NOT divisible by* 3.　　$7 \div 3 = 2$ *remainder* 1

estimate

An educated guess.

*An estimate can be used when you don't need an exact answer.
A good estimate for* 9.98×2 *is* 20 *because* $10 \times 2 = 20$.

expanded form

A way to write numbers using base 10.

You rewrite the digits with the proper place value. For 345,
hundreds　　　tens　　　ones
3　　　　　　　4　　　　　5

$3 \times 100 + 4 \times 10 + 5 \times 1$
$3 \times 10^2 + 4 \times 10^1 + 5 \times 10^0$
Expanded form uses base 10.

exponent

Tells how many times a base is used as a factor.

3^4 ← *The **exponent** is 4.*

The base 3 is used as a factor 4 times.

$3^4 = 3 \times 3 \times 3 \times 3 = 81$

Number Sense & Operations

factor

A number that is multiplied by another number to find a product.

3 and 4 are factors of 12.
3 × 4 = 12

factor tree

A diagram that shows the prime factors of a number.

There may be more than one factor tree for a number.

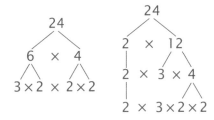

fraction

A number in the form $\frac{a}{b}$, where b cannot be equal to zero.

Fractions are usually used to compare a number of parts to the whole.

$$\frac{1}{2}, -\frac{5}{6}, \frac{x}{4} \text{ are all fractions.}$$

greatest

The largest number or quantity.

25, 8, 16
25 is the greatest number.

Data Analysis & Probability

Geometry & Measurement

Number Sense & Operations

Ratio, Proportion, & Percent

Equations & Inequalities

Variables & Expressions

Coordinate Plane

Reference Chart

greatest common factor

The common factor that is greater than any other common factor.

The greatest common factor is often abbreviated as GCF.

> *Factors of 12: 1, 2, 3, 4, 6, 12*
> *Factors of 8: 1, 2, 4, 8*
> *The common factors of 12 and 8 are: 1, 2, 4*
> *The greatest common factor of 12 and 8 is 4.*

Identity Property of One for Multiplication

The product of any number and one is that number.

This property is written algebraically as:
$5 \times 1 = 5$ $a \times 1 = a \ or \ 1 \times a = a.$
$1 \times 24 = 24$
$356 \times 1 = 356$

Identity Property of Zero for Addition

The sum of any number and zero is that number.

$5 + 0 = 5$ *This property is written algebraically as:*
$0 + 12 = 12$ $a + 0 = a \ or \ 0 + a = a.$
$276 + 0 = 276$

improper fraction

A fraction in which the numerator is greater than or equal to the denominator.

$\dfrac{12}{8}$ *is an improper fraction.* $\dfrac{7}{7}$ *is an improper fraction.*

$12 > 8$ $7 = 7$

Data Analysis & Probability

Geometry & Measurement

Number Sense & Operations

Ratio, Proportion, & Percent

Equations & Inequalities

Variables & Expressions

Coordinate Plane

Reference Chart

Number Sense & Operations

integers

The set of positive whole numbers, their opposites, and 0.

The set of integers is:
$\{..., -4, -3, -2, -1, 0, 1, 2, 3, 4, ...\}$

inverse operations

Any pair of operations that undo each other.

Inverse operations:

addition and subtraction	multiplication and division
$3 + 4 = 7$	$5 \times 2 = 10$
$7 - 4 = 3$	$10 \div 2 = 5$

irrational numbers

Numbers that cannot be written as the ratio of two integers.

In decimal form, an irrational number cannot be written as a decimal that repeats or ends.

π *and* $\sqrt{2}$ *are irrational numbers.*
$\pi = 3.1415926.....$ $\sqrt{2} = 1.4142135.....$
Approximations for π *and* $\sqrt{2}$ *are:*
$\pi \approx 3.14$ $\sqrt{2} \approx 1.41$

least

The smallest number or quantity.

16, 8, 3, 7
3 is the least number.

Data Analysis & Probability

Geometry & Measurement

Number Sense & Operations

Ratio, Proportion, & Percent

Equations & Inequalities

Variables & Expressions

Coordinate Plane

Reference Chart

Data Analysis & Probability

Geometry & Measurement

Number Sense & Operations

Ratio, Proportion, & Percent

Equations & Inequalities

Variables & Expressions

Coordinate Plane

Reference Chart

least common denominator

Least common multiple of the denominators of two or more fractions. LCD is often used as an abbreviation for the least common denominator.

$$\frac{5}{6} \quad \frac{9}{10} \quad \frac{2}{15}$$

In the example, the denominators are 6, 10, and 15.
Multiples of 6: 6, 12, 18, 24, 30, 36, 42, 48, 54, 60...
Multiples of 10: 10, 20, 30, 40, 50, 60...
Multiples of 15: 15, 30, 45, 60...
The least common denominator is 30 because the least common multiple is 30.

least common multiple

The common multiple that is less than any other common multiple of two or more numbers. The least common multiple is abbreviated as LCM.

Multiples:
8: 8, 16, 24, 32, 40, 48, ...
12: 12, 24, 36, 48, ...
Common multiples: 24, 48
LCM: 24

mixed number

A number that is formed with an integer and a fraction.

$$integer \longrightarrow 3\frac{1}{2} \longleftarrow fraction$$

All of the following are mixed numbers.

$$3\frac{1}{2}, \ 14\frac{1}{5}, \ 5\frac{7}{10}, \ -1\frac{3}{4}$$

multiple

A product of natural numbers.

$3 \times 4 = 12$ 12 *is a multiple of* 3 *and* 4.
$5 \times 6 = 30$ 30 *is a multiple of* 5 *and* 6.

natural numbers

Set of numbers you use to count.

$\{1, 2, 3, 4, 5, ...\}$
Natural numbers are also known as counting numbers.

numerator

The top number of a fraction. $\dfrac{2}{5}$ ←*numerator*

numerical expression

An expression with only numbers and one or more operation symbols.

$3 + 4$
$4 \times 3 \div 6$
$(6 + 5) \times 8 - 25$

opposite

A number that is the same distance from zero on a number line as a given number, but on the other side of zero.

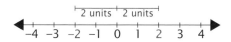

−2 *and* 2 *are opposites.*
−2 *is the opposite of* 2.
2 *is the opposite of* −2.

Data Analysis & Probability

Geometry & Measurement

Number Sense & Operations

Ratio, Proportion, & Percent

Equations & Inequalities

Variables & Expressions

Coordinate Plane

Reference Chart

Data Analysis & Probability

Geometry & Measurement

Number Sense & Operations

Ratio, Proportion, & Percent

Equations & Inequalities

Variables & Expressions

Coordinate Plane

Reference Chart

order of operations

A list of steps used to calculate an answer.

Order:
>*Parentheses*
>*Exponents*
>*Multiplication or Division (left to right)*
>*Addition or Subtraction (left to right)*

$4^2 - (5 - 2) \times 2 + 1$				
$4^2 -$	3	$\times 2 + 1$		*Parentheses*
$16 -$	3	$\times 2 + 1$		*Exponents*
$16 -$		6	$+ 1$	*Multiplication*
	10		$+ 1$	*Subtraction (occurs before addition, reading left to right)*
	11			*Addition*

pattern

An arrangement of numbers or things that can be described.

Some patterns:
>□, ▲, ○, □, ▲, ○...*(square, triangle, circle)*
>2, 4, 6, 8, 10...*(even counting numbers)*
>x, x^2, x^3, x^4...*(powers of x)*

perfect square

A number that has exactly two integer factors that are the same.

>4, 9, 16, 25, 36, 49, 64, 81, *and* 100 *are perfect squares.*

>$8 \times 8 = 64$, *so 64 is a perfect square.*

place value

Value of a digit in a number, based on the location of the digit.

9463.07

The value of 4 is 400 (4 hundred) because 4 is in the hundreds place.

power

An expression formed by a base with its exponent, or the value of that expression.

$3^2 = 9$
3^2 *is read "three to the second power" or "three squared;"*
9 *is the second power of three.*

prime factorization

Writing a composite number as the product of all of its prime factors.

$12 = 2 \times 2 \times 3 = 2^2 \times 3$
$39 = 3 \times 13$
$45 = 3 \times 3 \times 5 = 3^2 \times 5$
$16 = 2 \times 2 \times 2 \times 2 = 2^4$

prime number

Any whole number with exactly two different factors, 1 and itself.

Prime numbers are circled.

1 ②③ 4 ⑤
6 ⑦ 8 9 10
⑪ 12 ⑬ 14 15
16 ⑰ 18 ⑲ 20
21 22 ㉓ 24 25

Data Analysis & Probability

Geometry & Measurement

Number Sense & Operations

Ratio, Proportion, & Percent

Equations & Inequalities

Variables & Expressions

Coordinate Plane

Reference Chart

product

The answer to a multiplication problem.

$$3 \times 4 = 12$$

$\uparrow$
product

proper fraction

A fraction that is less than 1.

$\frac{2}{3}$ *and* $\frac{4}{5}$ *are proper fractions.*

quotient

The answer to a division problem.

$$\frac{4}{2\overline{)8}} \longleftarrow \textit{quotient}$$

rational numbers

Numbers that can be written as a fraction using two integers where the denominator is not 0.

Some rational numbers are:

$4, 0.75, -2\frac{1}{2}, 5.1, 0, 0.\overline{3}, \sqrt{4}$

$$4 = \frac{4}{1}$$

$$0.75 = \frac{3}{4}$$

$$-2\frac{1}{2} = \frac{5}{2}$$

$$5.1 = 5\frac{1}{10} = \frac{51}{10}$$

$$0 = \frac{0}{1}$$

$$0.\overline{3} = 0.333... = \frac{1}{3}$$

$$\sqrt{4} = \frac{2}{1}$$

real numbers

The set of numbers that includes all rational and irrational numbers.

Examples of Real Numbers:

$$0.\overline{3}, \pi, -5, 2\frac{5}{12}, -0.95, \sqrt{2}$$

reciprocals

Two numbers that when multiplied give a product of 1.

$$\frac{2}{1} \times \frac{1}{2} = 1 \qquad\qquad -\frac{2}{3} \times -\frac{3}{2} = 1$$

$\frac{1}{2}$ *and* 2 *are reciprocals.* $-\frac{2}{3}$ *and* $-\frac{3}{2}$ *are reciprocals.*

relatively prime numbers

Any two numbers whose greatest common factor is 1.

Factors of 27: 1, 3, 9, 27
Factors of 35: 1, 5, 7, 35

Greatest Common Factor = 1
27 and 35 are relatively prime.

repeating decimal

Any decimal that has one or more digits that repeat forever.

A single digit or set of repeating digits can be shown with a bar.

$$0.333... = 0.\overline{3}$$
$$0.4545... = 0.\overline{45}$$
$$0.625625625... = 0.\overline{625}$$

Data Analysis & Probability

Geometry & Measurement

Number Sense & Operations

Ratio, Proportion, & Percent

Equations & Inequalities

Variables & Expressions

Coordinate Plane

Reference Chart

scientific notation

A shorthand way of writing very large or very small numbers. A number written as a product so that the first factor is greater than 1 and less than 10, and the second factor is a power of 10.

$$8 \times 10^4$$

$$80,000$$
$$\downarrow$$
$$8 \times 10,000$$
$$\downarrow$$
$$\underbrace{8} \times \underbrace{10^4}$$
$$\uparrow \qquad \uparrow$$

first factor   second factor

To write 80,000 in scientific notation, first rewrite it in expanded form: 8 x 10,000.

Continue using a power of 10.

sequence

An ordered set of numbers.

1, 2, 3, 4, ...
–4, –2, 0, 2, 4, ...

simplest form (of a fraction)

A fraction written so that the numerator and denominator have no common factors other than 1.

$\frac{3}{12}$ *is not in simplest form.*

3 and 12 have a common factor of 3.

$$\frac{3}{12} = \frac{3 \div 3}{12 \div 3} = \frac{1}{4}$$

$\frac{1}{4}$ *is the simplest form of* $\frac{3}{12}$.

Data Analysis & Probability

Geometry & Measurement

Number Sense & Operations

Ratio, Proportion, & Percent

Equations & Inequalities

Variables & Expressions

Coordinate Plane

Reference Chart

Number Sense & Operations

simplify

To rewrite something in its simplest form.

Simplify: $3 \times 8 - 2$

Simplest form: 22

Simplify: $\frac{12}{14}$

$$\frac{12}{14} = \frac{6}{7}$$

Simplest form: $\frac{6}{7}$

square root

One of two equal factors of a number.

The symbol for square root is $\sqrt{}$.

$25 = 5 \times 5$, so the square root of 25 is 5. $\sqrt{25} = 5$.
$\sqrt{4} = 2$, $\sqrt{36} = 6$, $\sqrt{64} = 8$, $\sqrt{100} = 10$

standard form

A way of writing a number using digits and place value.

Everyday numbers like the ones below are written in standard form.

0.258
3.1
25
2,457,598

sum

The answer to an addition problem.

$$3 + 5 = 8$$
$$\uparrow$$
$$sum$$

Data Analysis & Probability

Geometry & Measurement

Number Sense & Operations

Ratio, Proportion, & Percent

Equations & Inequalities

Variables & Expressions

Coordinate Plane

Reference Chart

Data Analysis & Probability

Geometry & Measurement

Number Sense & Operations

Ratio, Proportion, & Percent

Equations & Inequalities

Variables & Expressions

Coordinate Plane

Reference Chart

term (of a pattern)

A number in a pattern.

> 1, 2, 4, 8, 16, ...
> *Each of the numbers listed above is a term.*

terminating decimal

A decimal that ends.

0.548
0.1
2.375

whole numbers

Zero and all the natural numbers.

> *The set of whole numbers is*
> $\{0,1,2,3,4...\}$.

Zero Property of Multiplication

The product of any number and zero is zero.

$3 \times 0 = 0$
$0 \times 156 = 0$

This property is written algebraically as:

$a \times 0 = 0$ *or* $0 \times a = 0$

Ratio, Proportion, & Percent

cross product

The product of two numbers that are diagonal from each other in a ratio.

$$\frac{3}{4} \times \frac{9}{12} \qquad \frac{x}{4} \times \frac{7}{2}$$

$$3 \times 12 = 4 \times 9 \qquad 2(x) = 4 \times 7$$
$$x = 14$$

discount

The amount subtracted from the price of an item.

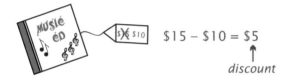

$15 − $10 = $5
↑
discount

equivalent fractions

Fractions that have the same value.

Equivalent Fractions   *NOT Equivalent Fractions*

$$\frac{3}{12}, \frac{25}{100} \qquad\qquad \frac{3}{5}, \frac{12}{24}$$

both equal $\frac{1}{4}$.

$$\frac{3}{12} \div \frac{3}{3} = \frac{1}{4} \qquad\qquad \frac{12}{24} = \frac{1}{2}$$

$$\frac{25}{100} \div \frac{25}{25} = \frac{1}{4} \qquad\qquad \frac{3}{5} \neq \frac{1}{2}$$

Data Analysis & Probability

Geometry & Measurement

Number Sense & Operations

Ratio, Proportion, & Percent

Equations & Inequalities

Variables & Expressions

Coordinate Plane

Reference Chart

interest

The amount paid for borrowing money or earned by lending money.

You pay interest on a loan, but you earn interest from money in a savings account.

percent

A ratio that compares a number to 100.

The symbol for percent is %. "Per" means "for" and "cent" means "hundred." 72% is read seventy-two percent and means 72 per 100 or 72/100.

principal

An amount of money borrowed or deposited.

When you put $100.00 in the bank for savings, the $100.00 is the principal.

When you borrow $15,000 to buy a car, the $15,000 is the principal.

proportion

An equation showing that two ratios are equal.

$$\frac{1}{2} = \frac{4}{8}$$

$$\frac{x}{25} = \frac{3}{5}$$

rate

A ratio that compares two quantities measured in different units.

25 miles in 4 hours   50 words per minute   7 points/game

Ratio, Proportion, & Percent

ratio

A comparison of two quantities using division.

There are 3 ways to show ratio:

3 *to* 5	3:5	$\frac{3}{5}$
the word "*to*"	*a colon* (:)	*a fraction*

scale

A ratio that compares dimensions in a drawing to the actual dimension.

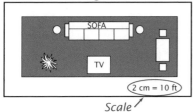

The scale of the living room drawing is 2 cm = 10 ft.

scale drawing

A drawing that shows a real object smaller than or larger than the actual object. Uses a scale to show size relationships.

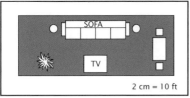

Data Analysis & Probability

Geometry & Measurement

Number Sense & Operations

Ratio, Proportion, & Percent

Equations & Inequalities

Variables & Expressions

Coordinate Plane

Reference Chart

 Ratio, Proportion, & Percent

scale model

A model of a real object that is smaller than or larger than the actual object.

Dollhouses and toy cars are scale models.

unit rate

A rate in which the number in the denominator is one.

$$\frac{65 \text{ miles}}{1 \text{ hour}}, \quad \frac{85 \text{ words}}{1 \text{ minute}}, \quad \frac{15 \text{ feet}}{1 \text{ second}}$$

Data Analysis & Probability

Geometry & Measurement

Number Sense & Operations

Ratio, Proportion, & Percent

Equations & Inequalities

Variables & Expressions

Coordinate Plane

Reference Chart

Equations & Inequalities

Addition Property of Equality

If the same number is added to each side of an equation, the results are equal.

The property is written in algebraic form for all numbers

a, b, and c: if $a = b$, then $a + c = b + c$.

$$3 = 3$$
$$3 + 4 = 3 + 4$$
$$7 = 7$$

If $a = b$, then $a + 2 = b + 2$.

$$a = b$$

$$a + 2 = b + 2$$

Division Property of Equality

If you divide each side of an equation by the same nonzero number, the sides remain equal.

The property is written in algebraic form for all numbers

a, b, and c, and c does not equal 0: if $a = b$, then $\frac{a}{c} = \frac{b}{c}$.

$$12 = 12$$
$$12 \div 3 = 12 \div 3$$
$$4 = 4$$

If then

$$3x = 24$$
$$\frac{3x}{3} = \frac{24}{3}$$
$$x = 8$$

Division Property of Equality

Data Analysis & Probability

Geometry & Measurement

Number Sense & Operations

Ratio, Proportion, & Percent

Equations & Inequalities

Variables & Expressions

Coordinate Plane

Reference Chart

Data Analysis & Probability

Geometry & Measurement

Number Sense & Operations

Ratio, Proportion, & Percent

Equations & Inequalities

Variables & Expressions

Coordinate Plane

Reference Chart

equation

A mathematical statement stating that two quantities are equal.

The symbol = is called the equal sign and is read "equals" or "is equal to."

$2 + 1 = 3$

$3x + 6 = 12$

$2(a + b) = 3c + 4d$

formula

A rule that shows a relationship between quantities.

A is area; l is length; w is width

Area = length x width

A = lw is a formula for the area of a rectangle.

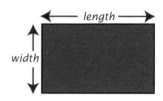

inequality

A mathematical sentence that uses one of the following symbols to state a relationship between two quantities:

< *is less than*		$3 + x < 5$ *3 plus x is less than 5.*
> *is greater than*		$4 \geq -2$ *4 is greater than or equal to –2.*
≤ *is less than or equal to*		
≥ *is greater than or equal to*		$3 \leq 3$ *3 is less than or equal to 3.*
≠ *is not equal to*		$7 \neq 6$ *7 is not equal to 6.*

Equations & Inequalities

Multiplication Property of Equality

If each side of an equation is multiplied by the same number, the sides remain equal.

The property is written in algebraic form for all numbers a, b, and c: if $a = b$, then $a \times c = b \times c$.

$$2 = 2 \qquad\qquad \frac{x}{2} = 5$$

$$2 \times 3 = 2 \times 3 \qquad 2\left(\frac{x}{2}\right) = 2(5)$$

solution

Any value that makes an equation or inequality true.

$x + 2 = 6$
$4 + 2 = 6$
4 is a solution of the equation.
$x + 2 = 6$ *because* $4 + 2 = 6$.
$y > 0$

5, 8, and 10 are some of the solutions of the inequality $y > 0$ because 5, 8, and 10 are all greater than 0. Other solutions include any number greater than 0. There are infinitely many solutions.

Subtraction Property of Equality

If the same number is subtracted from each side of an equation, the results are equal.

The property is written in algebraic form for all numbers a, b, and c: if $a = b$, then $a - c = b - c$.

$$8 = 8$$
$$8 - 2 = 8 - 2$$
$$6 = 6$$

$$\frac{a = b}{\blacktriangle}$$

$$\frac{a - 5 = b - 5}{\blacktriangle}$$

Data Analysis & Probability

Geometry & Measurement

Number Sense & Operations

Ratio, Proportion, & Percent

Equations & Inequalities

Variables & Expressions

Coordinate Plane

Reference Chart

Data Analysis & Probability

Geometry & Measurement

Number Sense & Operations

Ratio, Proportion, & Percent

Equations & Inequalities

Variables & Expressions

Coordinate Plane

Reference Chart

algebraic expression

An expression with only numbers, variables, operation symbols, and no equal sign.

$$9x^2 - 18x + 1$$
$$1 + \frac{a}{2}$$

binomial

A polynomial with only two terms.

$$x + 4$$
$$2y + 3z$$

coefficient

A number that is multiplied by a variable.

$$9x^2 - 18x + 1$$
$9, -18,$ *and* 1 *are all coefficients.*

like terms

Terms with the same variable factors.

Like terms:	*Not like terms:*
$9x^2, 2x^2$	$9x^2, 18x$

x is squared in the first term, but not in the second term.

Variables & Expressions

monomial

A number, variable, or a product of numbers and variables.

$3, x, -2y, \frac{1}{2}, a^2b$

polynomial

A monomial or sum or difference of monomials.

$$11x^2 - 18x + 1$$

simplify (an algebraic expression)

To rewrite an expression so that it has the fewest terms possible.

Simplify:
$$2x + 3x + 5y - 3y =$$
$$5x + 2y$$

term (of a polynomial)

A monomial in a polynomial.

In the polynomial:
$9x^2 - 18x + 1$,
$9x^2, -18x,$ *and* 1 *are all terms.*

variable

A letter used to represent one or more numbers.
The letters x and a are variables.

Data Analysis & Probability

Geometry & Measurement

Number Sense & Operations

Ratio, Proportion, & Percent

Equations & Inequalities

Variables & Expressions

Coordinate Plane

Reference Chart

Data Analysis & Probability

Geometry & Measurement

Number Sense & Operations

Ratio, Proportion, & Percent

Equations & Inequalities

Variables & Expressions

Coordinate Plane

Reference Chart

coordinate plane

A plane that is organized by a horizontal number line called the *x*-axis and a vertical number line called the *y*-axis.

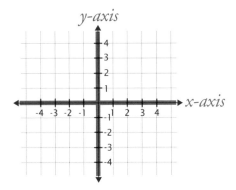

coordinates

The numbers in an ordered pair that tell the location of a point on the coordinate plane. For example, the coordinates for the ordered pair (2, 3) are 2 and 3.

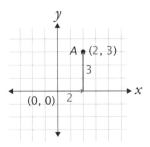

First coordinate—tells how far to move left or right from the origin.

↓

(2, 3)

↑

Second coordinate—tells how far to move up or down from the origin.

Coordinate Plane

function

A relationship of inputs and outputs so that there is exactly one output for each input.

Example 1

input	output
7	10
8	11
12	15
2	5

Function

input	output
2	6
4	5
2	8
9	7

Not a Function

Example 2

At $8 an Hour	
Hours Worked (h)	Paid (p)
2	$16
3	$24
4	$32

The second table is NOT a function because there are two different outputs (6 and 8) for the input 2.

The number of hours you are paid (p) is a function of hours worked (h). There is exactly one dollar amount (output, p) for each hour worked (input, h).

linear function

A function that has the shape of a line when graphed on the coordinate plane.

Function: $y = 2x + 1$

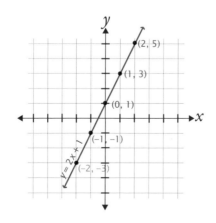

Data Analysis & Probability

Geometry & Measurement

Number Sense & Operations

Ratio, Proportion, & Percent

Equations & Inequalities

Variables & Expressions

Coordinate Plane

Reference Chart

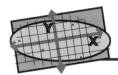

ordered pair

A pair of numbers that gives the position of a point on the coordinate plane.

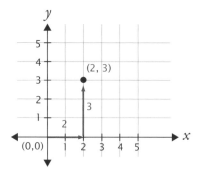

(2, 3) *is an ordered pair.*

origin

The point where the *x*-axis and *y*-axis of a coordinate plane cross.

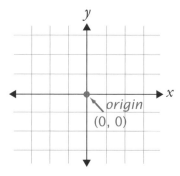

64

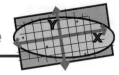

quadrant

The four sections of the coordinate plane.

Quadrants are numbered with Roman numerals (I, II, III, IV).

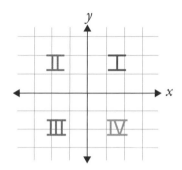

reflection

A transformation that flips a figure over a line to produce a mirror image.

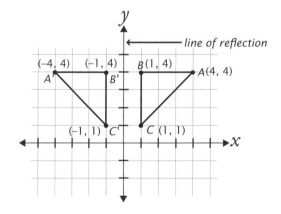

Data Analysis & Probability

Geometry & Measurement

Number Sense & Operations

Ratio, Proportion, & Percent

Equations & Inequalities

Variables & Expressions

Coordinate Plane

Reference Chart

Data Analysis & Probability

Geometry & Measurement

Number Sense & Operations

Ratio, Proportion, & Percent

Equations & Inequalities

Variables & Expressions

Coordinate Plane

Reference Chart

rotation

A transformation that turns a figure about a fixed point.

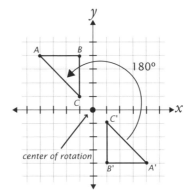

slope

A ratio that describes the steepness of a line in the coordinate plane.

Slope is represented by the variable m and is often referred to as "rise over run."

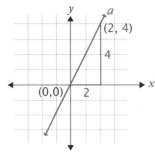

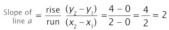

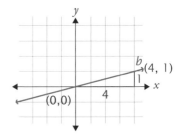

Slope of line a = $\dfrac{\text{rise}}{\text{run}}$ $\dfrac{(y_2 - y_1)}{(x_2 - x_1)}$ = $\dfrac{4 - 0}{2 - 0}$ = $\dfrac{4}{2}$ = 2

Slope of line b = $\dfrac{\text{rise}}{\text{run}}$ $\dfrac{(y_2 - y_1)}{(x_2 - x_1)}$ = $\dfrac{1 - 0}{4 - 0}$ = $\dfrac{1}{4}$

The slope of line a is 2, which is greater than the slope of line b, $\dfrac{1}{4}$.

Line a is taller, or "steeper," than line b.
Slope measures the "steepness" of a line.

Coordinate Plane

slope-intercept form

A linear equation written in the form $y = mx + b$, where m represents slope and b represents the y-intercept.

$$y = mx + b$$

$$y = \frac{2}{3}\, x + 1$$
↑ slope   ↑ y-intercept

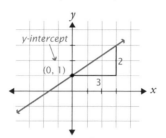

translation

A transformation that slides each point of a figure the same distance and in the same direction.

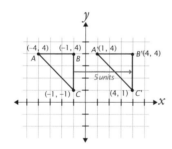

x-axis

The horizontal number line in the coordinate plane.

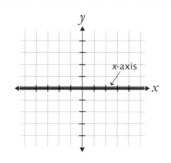

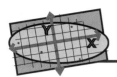

Coordinate Plane

x-coordinate

The first number in an ordered pair that tells how far from (0,0) to move left or right. In the ordered pair (2,3), 2 is the x-coordinate.

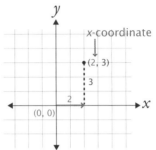

x-intercept

The x-coordinate of the point where a line crosses the x-axis.

The coordinates for the x-intercept are (–3,0).

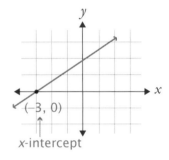

y-axis

The vertical number line in the coordinate plane.

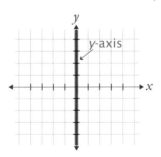

Data Analysis & Probability

Geometry & Measurement

Number Sense & Operations

Ratio, Proportion, & Percent

Equations & Inequalities

Variables & Expressions

Coordinate Plane

Reference Chart

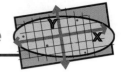

y-coordinate

The second number in an ordered pair that tells how far from (0,0) to move up or down. In the ordered pair (2,3), 3 is the y-coordinate.

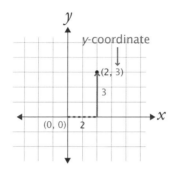

y-intercept

The y-coordinate of the point where a line crosses the y-axis.

The coordinates for the y-intercept are (0,2).

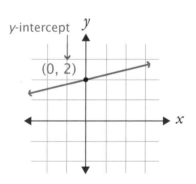

Data Analysis & Probability

Geometry & Measurement

Number Sense & Operations

Ratio, Proportion, & Percent

Equations & Inequalities

Variables & Expressions

Coordinate Plane

Reference Chart

Reference Chart

Data Analysis & Probability

Geometry & Measurement

Number Sense & Operations

Ratio, Proportion, & Percent

Equations & Inequalities

Variables & Expressions

Coordinate Plane

Reference Chart

LENGTH

Metric
1 kilometer = 1,000 meters
1 meter = 100 centimeters
1 centimeter = 10 millimeters

Customary
1 mile = 1,760 yards
1 mile = 5,280 feet
1 yard = 3 feet = 36 inches
1 foot = 12 inches

CAPACITY AND VOLUME

Metric
1 liter = 1,000 milliliters

Customary
1 cup = 8 ounces
1 pint = 2 cups
1 quart = 2 pints
1 gallon = 4 quarts

MASS AND WEIGHT

Metric
1 gram = 1,000 milligrams
1 kilogram = 1,000 grams

Customary
1 pound = 16 ounces
1 ton = 2,000 pounds

TIME

1 minute = 60 seconds
1 hour = 60 minutes
1 year = 12 months

1 week = 7 days
1 day = 24 hours
1 year = 365 days

Reference Chart

Perimeter

square

 s

$$P = 4s$$

rectangle

 w

l

$$P = 2l + 2w \quad or \quad P = 2(l + w)$$

Circumference

circle

 r

$$C = 2\pi r \quad or \quad C = \pi d$$

Area

square

 s

s

$$A = s^2$$

rectangle

 w

l

$$A = lw$$

parallelogram

 h

b

$$A = bh$$

Data Analysis & Probability

Geometry & Measurement

Number Sense & Operations

Ratio, Proportion, & Percent

Equations & Inequalities

Variables & Expressions

Coordinate Plane

Reference Chart

Reference Chart

Area (continued)

triangle

$$A = \frac{1}{2}bh \quad or \quad A = \frac{bh}{2}$$

trapezoid

$$A = \frac{1}{2}h\,(b_1 + b_2)$$

circle

$$A = \pi r^2$$

Volume

cube

Surface Area

$$V = s^3 \qquad S.A. = 6s^2$$

rectangular prism

Surface Area

$$V = lwh$$

$$S.A. = 2(lw) + 2(hw) + 2(lh)$$

circular cylinder

Surface Area

$$V = \pi r^2 h \qquad S.A. = 2\pi rh + 2\pi r^2$$

Reference Chart

Pi

$$\pi \qquad \pi \approx 3.14 \quad or \quad \pi \approx \frac{22}{7}.$$

Degree (temperature)

$F = \frac{9}{5}C + 32$

$C = \frac{5}{9}(F - 32)$

°C °F
0° 32°
    0°

A unit used to measure temperature.

Different scales like Celsius and Fahrenheit can be used to measure temperature.

The temperature on this thermometer is 0°C or 32°F.

Data Analysis & Probability

Geometry & Measurement

Number Sense & Operations

Ratio, Proportion, & Percent

Equations & Inequalities

Variables & Expressions

Coordinate Plane

Reference Chart

Index

Index

Index

Notes

Notes

Notes

Notes

Notes

Notes